DAT

The Tuskegee Airmen

LINDA AND CHARLES GEORGE

CHILDREN'S PRESS®

A Division of Grolier Publishing

New York • London • Hong Kong • Sydney

Danbury, Connecticut

Reading Consultant: Linda Cornwell, Coordinator of School Quality and Professional Improvement Indiana State Teachers Association

Content Consultant: Dr. Alan L. Gropman, Industrial College of the Armed Forces

Visit Children's Press on the Internet at:
http://publishing.grolier.com

Library of Congress Cataloging-in-Publication Data

George, Linda.
    The Tuskegee Airmen / Linda and Charles George.
        p. cm.—(Cornerstones of freedom)
    Includes index.
    ISBN 0-516-21602-3 (lib. bdg.)   ISBN 0-516-27280-2 (pbk.)
    1. World War, 1939–1945—Aerial operations, American—Juvenile
literature. 2. Afro-American air pilots—History—Juvenile works.
3. World War, 1939–1945—Participation, Afro-American—Juvenile
literature. 4. Tuskegee Army Air Field (Ala.)—Juvenile literature.
[1. World War 1939–1945—Aerial operations. 2. World War
1939–1945—Participation, Afro-American.] I. George, Charles,
1949– II. Title. III. Series.
D798.G46 2001
940.54'4973—dc21
                                                00-024020

When the United States was involved in World War II (1941–1945), African-American pilots trained at Tuskegee Army Air Field near Tuskegee, Alabama. These pilots were known by several names. Because they learned to fly near Tuskegee, many people called them the "Tuskegee Airmen." Germans called them "Black Birdmen." The African-American pilots provided protection for American bomber pilots and crews on bombing runs. When the Tuskegee Airmen began flying planes with red tails, the people who depended on them for protection called them the "Red-Tailed Angels."

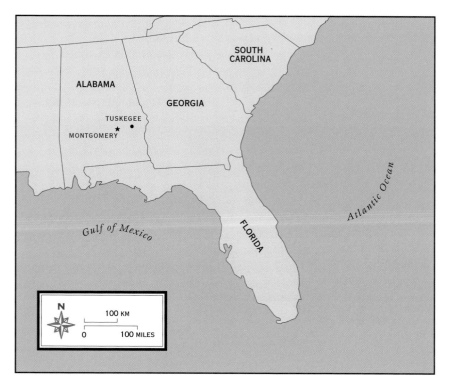

Tuskegee, Alabama, is located between the capital city of Montgomery and the Georgia border.

Whatever their nickname, the Tuskegee Airmen were known for their courage, discipline, and exceptional skill as pilots. During the early and mid 1900s, most whites in the United States government were determined to segregate, or separate, blacks from whites in the military. Despite this discrimination, the Tuskegee Airmen fought bravely and helped to preserve freedom for all.

From the beginning of the U.S. Army Air Service in 1907, African-Americans were not admitted to flying programs. This discrimination increased when the Army War College issued a racially biased report in 1925. This report was based largely on personal opinions rather than facts. The report stated that as a race, blacks were not as smart as whites. In addition, the report said African-Americans did not have the courage to fight in battle. Army officials used the report to prevent African-Americans

This photograph of the Army War College was taken in 1927.

from serving in the military except in unskilled positions—such as busboys, kitchen help, construction workers, truck drivers, or dockworkers.

Most army officials believed African-Americans lacked the ability to operate machinery as complicated as aircraft. So African-Americans in the U.S. armed forces were not given opportunities in aviation—the operation of heavier-than-air aircraft. Many people wrongly considered African-Americans untrustworthy and lazy. Others thought African-Americans did not have the leadership qualities needed to serve as military officers.

Despite the army officials' low opinion of African-American pilots, they had been flying for years. Bessie Coleman, Willa Brown, Cornelius Coffee, Dr. Albert E. Forsythe, and Charles Alfred Anderson were only a few of the African-Americans who learned to fly. They fought discrimination and segregation to become pilots. One African-American pilot, Eugene Jacques Bullard, flew with the French air force in World War I (1914–1918).

Bessie Coleman was the first African-American woman aviator. She earned her wings in Paris, and she performed in air shows across the United States during the 1920s.

Franklin Delano Roosevelt

The opportunity for African-American pilots to serve in the U.S. military improved in the late 1930s, when President Franklin Delano Roosevelt started building up the U.S. armed forces. Germany and Italy had invaded weaker countries and agreed to support one another's policies. President Roosevelt was looking for ways to provide more military protection for the United States in case of war. One idea was to train civilians—people who are not in the armed forces—to fly. In April 1939, Congress passed a law that allowed civilian aviation schools to train pilots. This program, the Civilian Pilot Training Program (CPTP), provided training for twenty thousand college students yearly as private pilots. Soon the law changed, allowing the secretary of war to lend equipment to schools for African-American pilot training.

While the CPTP was in the works, Edgar G. Brown, an African-American spokesman for government employees, arranged an unusual flight. Two African-American pilots from the National Airmen's Association, Dale White and Chauncey Spencer, flew from Chicago, Illinois, to Washington, D.C. Their plane was a single-engine, propeller-driven biplane—a plane with two wings, one above the other. In Washington, White and Spencer met with Harry S. Truman on May 9, 1939. At that time, Truman was a senator from Missouri.

Since aviation was still relatively new, and the small plane so poorly equipped, White and Spencer's achievement impressed Senator Truman. He told them, "If you guys had guts enough to fly that [airplane] from Chicago, I got guts enough to do all I can to help you." Senator Truman—along with African-American leaders Walter White, A. Philip Randolph, and Mary McLeod Bethune—pressured Congress until additional funds were provided for training African-American pilots. Congress also might have been persuaded to act because of the worsening situation in Europe. Germany invaded Poland, and Great Britain and France declared war on Germany on September 3, 1939.

Congress approved the needed training sites for the CPTP. West Virginia State College was named as a training site. Soon, the University of West Virginia, North Carolina Agricultural & Technical College, Howard University, Delaware State, Hampton Institute, and the Tuskegee Institute were also approved.

This photograph of the chapel at the Tuskegee Institute was taken in 1937.

African-American leader and educator Booker T. Washington had founded the Tuskegee Institute in 1881. In 1940, Dr. Frederick Patterson was president of the Tuskegee Institute, and he wanted its CPTP program to succeed. To insure the best pilot instruction, he hired Charles Anderson to head the training. Although Anderson was a self-taught pilot, he was known for his accomplishments. In 1929, he became the first African-American to earn a private pilot's license in the United States. Later, he was one of the first African-Americans to fly across the United States.

On July 29, 1940, Anderson, later nicknamed "Chief," arrived at the Tuskegee Institute in a new 225-horsepower airplane—a Waco trainer—painted Army Air Corps blue and yellow. At first, pilot trainees at Tuskegee had to make 40-mile (64-kilometer) round-trips to an airport in Montgomery, Alabama, for flight training. Later, they were taught at Kennedy Field, a grass strip volunteers built near the Institute.

A second airfield, Moton Field, was under construction, but the Tuskegee Institute was having trouble paying for it. In 1941, the Institute appealed to the Julius Rosenwald Fund of Chicago for financial help to complete Moton Field. The Fund's board of directors met at the Institute. Among those present was First Lady Eleanor Roosevelt. She opposed racial discrimination and supported African-Americans' rights. The First Lady came to the meeting to learn more about African-American pilots. She had a bold plan to prove that they could fly.

Arriving at Tuskegee on April 19, 1941, Eleanor Roosevelt surprised everyone by asking Chief Anderson to take her for an airplane ride. People did not expect a president's wife to take such spur-of-the-moment risks. Some board members and Secret Service agents assigned to protect her wanted to call the president to get him to stop her. Despite their protests, she climbed into the airplane, and she and Anderson took off. After a thirty-minute flight, Mrs.

By flying with Chief Anderson (right), Eleanor Roosevelt (left) showed people that African-Americans had the skills to be excellent pilots.

Roosevelt proudly proclaimed to the press, "Well, he can fly alright!" The First Lady's courage and support, and the fact that she publicly trusted her life to the skill of an African-American pilot, set an example. The Rosenwald Fund, known for giving money to help African-Americans, loaned the Institute $175,000 of the $200,000 it needed to complete Moton Field.

This photograph is an aerial view of Tuskegee Army Air Field in 1944.

The U.S. government paid for the construction of a third airfield 7 miles (11 km) northwest of the town of Tuskegee. The War Department had announced it would form an all-black fighter group, the 99th Pursuit Squadron. The group would train in Tuskegee, Alabama. Designed for combat training, the Tuskegee Army Air Field (TAAF) was completed in three months. On July 19, 1941, TAAF officially opened.

The first members of the 99th Pursuit Squadron arrived in October 1941, and combat flight training began. This first group consisted of twelve cadets and an officer trainee. Among the cadets were Charles DeBow, Mac Ross, George "Spanky" Roberts, and Lemuel Rodney Custis. The officer trainee was Benjamin O. Davis Jr. His father, Benjamin O. Davis Sr., was the army's only African-American general.

The younger Davis graduated from the U.S. Military Academy at West Point in 1936 despite considerable hardship. During his four years at the Point, white cadets refused to speak to him outside of official duties, a terrible tradition called "silencing." One military historian writes, "He had no roommate. . . . He had no groups with which to study, no partner with whom to share a pup tent." Although Benjamin O. Davis Jr. was lonely and faced discrimination, he would not be discouraged from his goal of becoming a pilot.

Now Davis and the cadets had to prove themselves fit for military duty as fighter pilots. If they succeeded, they would demonstrate the skill of their race. African-Americans dreamed of equality in a country that seemed determined to keep them oppressed and segregated. Racial segregation was the custom in the South. "Jim Crow" laws, named for a character in an old Southern song, separated blacks from whites in every aspect of life.

Blacks could not drink from the same drinking fountains as whites while Jim Crow laws were enforced.

African-Americans coming from the North to train in Tuskegee, Alabama, had to learn to live under Jim Crow laws. For many members of the 99th Squadron, dealing with segregation was a greater challenge than combat training. Most of them had taken classes at Chanute Field, in Rantoul, Illinois, where separation of the races was not as strictly enforced.

In 1942, an instructor at the Tuskegee Army Air Field teaches students how to send and receive Morse code, a means of radio communication that uses short and long tones.

The cadets knew they were considered second-class citizens outside their Alabama classroom, but flight training was a different story. Instructors set personal feelings aside when teaching cadets to fly. Equipment was well maintained and instruction proved to be excellent, giving cadets confidence and self-esteem. Training included 480 hours of classes on the ground and as many as 100 hours of flight instruction.

Benjamin O. Davis Jr. said, "The training at Tuskegee Army Air Field . . . was the equal of whatever was going on in . . . any other flying school operated by the Army Air Corps." As a result, black cadets who completed training were as capable as white pilots.

During training, the cadets were sometimes visited by African-American celebrities. Entertainers such as movie star and singer Lena Horne visited the base officers' club. As the first of their race to meet the challenge of learning to fly for the Army Air Corps, the Tuskegee Airmen were celebrities too.

Captain Davis had the honor of being the first African-American officer to solo in an Army Air Corps aircraft. Recalling the experience, he said, "I was alone in the air and that . . . was a thrill." Captain Davis's solo flight was also a thrill for cadets watching from the ground. He carried their hopes that black pilots would be accepted as equals and allowed to fly for the army alongside white pilots. That desire grew stronger on December 7, 1941, when Japanese forces attacked the U.S. Naval Base at Pearl Harbor, Hawaii. The next day, the United States entered World War II against Germany, Italy, and Japan.

Captain Benjamin Davis Jr. sits in the cockpit of an advanced trainer.

Americans had been at war for almost three months when the cadets made history at Tuskegee, Alabama, on March 7, 1942. Captain Davis and cadets DeBow, Ross, Roberts, and Custis graduated from pilot training and received their wings—a first for African-Americans. The four cadets became pilots and second lieutenants in the U.S. Army Air Force.

Colonel Noel F. Parrish

Captain Davis became commander of the 99th Squadron on August 24, 1942. In December, Colonel Noel F. Parrish became commander of TAAF. He thought the Tuskegee Airmen were making valuable contributions to a country desperately in need of fighter pilots. He also admired their dedication to their country, despite being treated poorly. Unlike other officers, Colonel Parrish attended the Tuskegee Airmen's social gatherings and got to know them personally. As a result, they respected and admired him.

By the end of 1942, the 99th Fighter Squadron (as it was now called) was ready to enter the war in Europe. Instead of being sent overseas, though, the Tuskegee Airmen were given extra training not required of white cadets. In February 1943, months after the 99th could have been sent into action, Secretary of War Henry Stimson visited TAAF. He declared the outfit as good as any he had seen, but the 99th was still not sent to fight.

On March 7, 1942, five men became the first African-American officers in the U.S. Army Air Force (from left to right): Second Lieutenant George Roberts, Captain Benjamin Davis, Second Lieutenant Charles DeBow, Lietenant R.M. Long (their instructor), Second Lieutenant Mac Ross, and Second Lieutenant Lemuel Rodney Custis.

Soon after Stimson's visit, Colonel Parrish went to Washington, D.C., to see Robert Lovett, the assistant secretary of war for air. Parrish insisted the 99th was ready for combat. His efforts, along with other supporters of the program—including Army Chief of Staff George Marshall—convinced the War Department to ship the Tuskegee Airmen overseas. Because of Colonel Parrish's continued encouragement, sensitivity, and support, the members of the 99th affectionately called him "the Great White Father."

At last, on April 15, 1943, the outfit shipped out to North Africa and was eventually stationed in Tunisia. A support crew, including technicians, flight surgeons, and nurses, accompanied the Tuskegee Airmen. Excited and happy, the pilots wanted to prove what they could do.

Once in North Africa, the Tuskegee Airmen had hoped to be far away from the racial problems they had faced in the United States. However, they were tightly segregated from white pilots. They were treated disrespectfully by the commander and members of the 33rd Fighter Group—the organization to which they were assigned. Yet the Tuskegee Airmen were determined to fight for their country no matter how anyone treated them.

On June 2, 1943, the 99th Fighter Squadron launched its first ground strafing attack—flying at low altitudes while shooting ground targets

16

with machine guns. The squadron's target was the heavily defended island of Pantelleria, halfway between Tunisia and Sicily. On July 2, while attacking the town of Casteveltrano, Sicily, Lieutenant Charles B. Hall scored the squadron's first victory. While he was escorting a B-25 bomber group, Hall shot down a German fighter plane.

The Tuskegee Airmen flew more than ten thousand missions over Europe during World War II. This map shows present-day countries and borders.

Triumph was mixed with tragedy, though. Hall learned that aircraft flown by fellow 99th Fighter Squadron pilots Sherman White Jr. and James McCullin had collided that morning, killing both men. Airplane accidents and combat losses deeply saddened the pilots. The empty feeling of losing a friend was magnified by the realization that they could die too.

In 1944, Lemuel Rodney Custis (left) and Charles B. Hall (right) talk while on leave. They used their time off to help the National Association for the Advancement of Colored People raise money for the war effort.

During the summer and fall of 1943, the 99th Fighter Squadron was assigned mainly to support operations. The Tuskegee Airmen's mission was to seek out fuel dumps, ammunition dumps, supply routes, trains, trucks, and tanks. They rarely encountered enemy aircraft. As a result, they had a poor record of downed enemy planes.

Army Air Force senior officers who did not want African-Americans pilots serving in the military used this record to discredit the Tuskegee Airmen. A commanding general of the Army Air Corps recommended removing the 99th from combat flying, assigning it to coastal patrol, and abandoning other Tuskegee Airmen units then in training. Davis, a colonel by this time, fought to keep his pilots in the air, and Army Chief of Staff George Marshall overruled the Air Corps general's recommendation.

In October 1943, the 99th Fighter Squadron was transferred to the 79th Fighter Group. No longer confined to strafing missions, the Tuskegee Airmen were treated as equals by Colonel Earl E. Bates. Black pilots flew in formation with white pilots. The Tuskegee Airmen enjoyed more acceptance and friendship while contributing to the war effort. Pilot Wilson V. Eagleson said of those days, "That was the most exciting time I [had while] I was overseas."

During January 1944, the squadron was part of the assault on the coastal city of Anzio, Italy. On January 27, eight pilots did victory rolls, signaling downed enemy planes. Lemuel Rodney Custis said, "Our squadron went from a squadron that had been ignored . . . to one recognized again because we had shot down some airplanes. And that was the turning point of the history and the fortunes of the 99th." Custis added, "The front pages [of African-American newspapers] belonged to the men shooting down airplanes."

During the three-day battle over Anzio, the Tuskegee Airmen destroyed seventeen German

On January 29, 1944, lieutenants in the 99th Fighter Squadron talk over the day's adventures in the sky.

aircraft. They proved that they were worthy to fly and fight. African-American pilots had earned their place in the war effort.

News of their excellence spread. In the spring of 1944, Colonel Davis, then commander of the 332nd Fighter Group, met with Army Air Corps General Ira C. Eaker. Bombers seeking to destroy German weapons and supplies were suffering heavy casualties. On some missions, the Americans and the British lost more than twenty-five bombers—each with a crew of eleven men—because the fighter escorts sent to protect the bombers often left their positions. The escorts took off to chase or even hunt enemy planes, seeking personal glory. General Eaker asked Colonel Davis if his pilots could provide the unselfish teamwork needed to protect the bomber crews. Davis assured the general he could count on the Tuskegee Airmen.

Colonel Davis recognized this opportunity as a way to further prove African-Americans' worth in combat. He told his pilots about their new assignment and warned them of severe penalties—grounding and court-martial—if anyone abandoned the bombers. In June 1944, the 99th Fighter Squadron joined the 332nd Fighter Group. During the first forty days of their escort operation, the 332nd shot down forty enemy planes without losing a single American or British bomber to enemy fighters.

During these missions, the Tuskegee Airmen flew Republic P-47 Thunderbolts. The pilots called the planes "Jugs." The P-47 could fly 412 miles (663 km) per hour at an altitude of more than 30,000 feet (9,000 meters). On June 9, 1944, escort planes from the 332nd approached Udine, Italy. Four enemy planes dived on the formation. Lieutenant Wendell Pruitt described the battle:

> *As the [Germans] passed under me I rolled over, shoved everything forward, dove and closed in on one [enemy plane] at 475 miles per hour. I gave him a short burst of machine-gun fire, found I was giving him too much lead, so I waited as he shallowed out of a turn. Then I gave two long, two-second bursts. I saw his left wing burst into flames. The plane exploded and went straight into the ground, but the pilot bailed out safely.*

Five enemy planes were shot down that day. But not every mission was successful. On June 22, 1944, Captain Robert B. Tresville, the commanding officer of the 100th Fighter Squadron, and two other pilots flew a mission to the island of Corsica. Trying to avoid being spotted, the formation flew low over the water under a solid cloud cover. The pilots became disoriented and crashed into the sea.

A Republic P-47 Thunderbolt

Lieutenants Wendell Pruitt and Guinn Pierson were determined not to let this tragedy stop them from doing their duty. Three days later, they sank a German destroyer off the coast of Italy. Using machine-gun fire, Pruitt and Pierson caused the ship's ammunition to explode. They also hit enemy targets in the Italian port city of Pesaro. Both pilots were awarded the Distinguished Flying Cross (DFC), an award for heroism or extraordinary achievement in flight, for sinking the German destroyer.

The Tuskegee Airmen came home with hundreds of awards, including many DFCs and one Silver Star. Their heroic missions continued in P-51 Mustangs, the Air Force's newest fighter—and its pride and joy. This plane could fly 10,000 feet (3,000 m) higher and 75 miles (120 km) per hour faster than the Jug. Proud of their new aircraft, the Tuskegee Airmen painted the tails of their planes bright red—leading to the nickname, the "Red-Tailed Angels."

Above: The Distinguished Flying Cross. Right: General Benjamin O. Davis Sr. (center right) pins the Distinguished Flying Cross on his son, Colonel Benjamin O. Davis Jr. (center left). Colonel Davis earned the award for his leadership and bravery during the June 9, 1944, mission.

A P-51 Mustang

George McGovern, an American bomber pilot who eventually became a senator and presidential candidate, recalled: "It was a wondrous sight to see those escort fighter planes coming up to take care of us, escorting us into the targets, picking us up after the bombing raid and taking us home. . . . The planes that the Tuskegee Airmen . . . flew . . . were marked with red tails so you couldn't miss them. They were flown by men with enormous skill and coordination."

White bomber groups knew the Red-Tailed Angels would not leave them, no matter how intense the air combat. They also knew no bomber escorted by the Tuskegee Airmen had ever been shot down. When faced with life or death issues, pilots learned the color of a person's skin meant nothing. Tuskegee Airman Wilson V. Eagleson said, "There's no such thing as segregation when you're fighting side by side."

On March 24, 1945, Davis led fifty-four pilots on an escort mission to Berlin, Germany. Not a single bomber was lost on the historic run. The 332nd Fighter Group was awarded the Presidential Distinguished Unit citation for the "gallantry, professional skill, and determination of the pilots" on the mission.

By the spring of 1945, the Tuskegee Airmen had downed 111 enemy aircraft and destroyed another 150 on the ground. They disabled more than six hundred boxcars, locomotives, tanks, and trucks. They sank one German destroyer and forty other boats and barges. On their best day, the Red-Tailed Angels shot down thirteen German fighters. On April 26, 1945, they shot down the last four enemy aircraft in combat over the Mediterranean.

Amazingly, the Tuskegee Airmen flew two hundred bomber escort missions without losing

Six P-51 Mustangs of the 332nd Fighter Group return to their home base in Italy after a bomber escort mission.

a single bomber to enemy attacks. Their record was never equaled by any other fighter group— white or black. But, along with victory came losses. Sixty-six Tuskegee Airmen were killed in action. Thirty-two were captured and became prisoners of war.

After Germany surrendered on May 8, 1945, the 332nd Fighter Group was disbanded. It was time for the Tuskegee Airmen to go home. Later that year, on August 14, Japan surrendered, ending World War II.

Despite their great achievements, the Tuskegee Airmen returned home to a country still intent on keeping them segregated and oppressed. After being recognized for their excellence, they found it extremely difficult to accept being treated as second-class citizens. They had tasted victory and would never again settle for less than equality.

President Harry S. Truman was inspired by the Tuskegee Airmen's magnificent contribution to the war effort. He kept his earlier promise to help African-American pilots. On July 26, 1948, the president announced Executive Order 9981, calling for "equality of treatment and opportunity" in the armed forces— regardless of race. The act led to the end of segregation in the armed forces. Even greater civil rights legislation would be enacted in the decades to follow.

Harry S. Truman

General Benjamin O. Davis Jr. (center) receives his fourth star on December 9, 1998. President Bill Clinton (left) wears an honorary red blazer that is the trademark of the Tuskegee Airmen. The president and Elnora Davis McLendon (right), General Davis's sister, pin the stars on General Davis.

Some Tuskegee Airmen stayed in the military, fighting in later wars. Benjamin O. Davis Jr. continued his rise through military rank to that of four-star general. President Bill Clinton bestowed this honor on Davis in 1998. At the ceremony, the president said Davis is "a hero in war, a leader in peace, [and] a pioneer for freedom, opportunity, and basic human dignity." Twenty former Tuskegee Airmen attended the ceremony.

Charles McGee also continued a distinguished military career spanning thirty years. In addition to fighting in World War II, he served in Korea and Vietnam. McGee achieved the highest three-war total of fighter missions of any Air Force aviator—409 missions. From 1983 to 1985 and again from 1998 to 2000, he served as national president of the Tuskegee Airmen Incorporated, founded in 1972.

Charles McGee

Former president of the Tuskegee Airmen Incorporated, Roger C. (Bill) Terry, describes the goals of the organization:

To let our children and our children's children know that we did conquer the art of flying and that we were able to do things that the [leaders of the U.S. armed forces] said we couldn't do. They said at the beginning of World War II that . . . [African-Americans] couldn't fly. We proved we could excel. We triumphed over the odds and we want to tell our youngsters to prepare themselves and to use their God-given talents . . . not only to fly airplanes, but to become doctors, lawyers, or rock singers if they want to . . . but not to let anyone tell them that they can't.

The Tuskegee Airmen fought for the country they loved, even when many citizens of that country expected them to fail. The Tuskegee Airmen proved those expectations wrong. Air Force Chief of Staff General Ronald R. Fogleman said, "In the end, the men and the women of the Tuskegee experience broke forever the myths that allowed segregation, [inequality], and injustice to exist. . . ." The victories of the Tuskegee Airmen led to the day when every citizen of the United States would have equal rights.

GLOSSARY

altitude – a height measured from sea level or from the earth's surface

aviation – the operation of heavier-than-air aircraft

bomber – a military airplane designed to carry and drop bombs

cadets

cadet – a person who is training to become a member of the armed forces with rank and authority

casualty; plural, **casualties** – a person who is injured or killed in an accident, a disaster, or a war

citizen – a person who is an official member of a political body, such as a country

civilian – someone who is not a member of the armed forces

combat – military conflict

court-martial – a trial involving members of the armed forces

discrimination – unjust behavior to others based on difference in age, race, or gender

escort – (noun) one or more planes traveling with another to give protection; (verb) to accompany for protection

formation – a specific arrangement of planes

grounding – preventing a pilot from flying

Jim Crow laws – laws enacted to segregate blacks from whites that were in effect in the United States for approximately one hundred years after the end of the Civil War

Jim Crow laws

oppress – to treat in a cruel and unjust way

segregate – to separate by race or ethnic background, keeping people apart from the main group

squadron – a group of ships, planes, troops, or other military units

strafing – attacking with machine-gun fire from low-flying aircraft

TIMELINE

1925

U.S. Army War College issues report that discriminates against African-Americans

President Franklin Delano Roosevelt builds up armed forces } **1938**

1939 Civilian Pilot Training Program established; World War II begins in Europe

1941

Eleanor Roosevelt visits Tuskegee Institute; first pilots arrive at Tuskegee; combat flight training begins; United States enters World War II

1942 { *March 7:* First class of Tuskegee Airmen graduates

1943 *April:* 99th Fighter Squadron heads for North Africa

1944

June: 99th joins 332nd Fighter Group under command of Colonel Davis; Pruitt and Pierson sink a German destroyer and earn Distinguished Flying Cross

March 24: Colonel Davis leads fifty-four pilots to Berlin; 332nd awarded Presidential Distinguished Unit citation

May 8: Germany surrenders; 332nd is disbanded

August 14: World War II ends with Japan's surrender

1945 *July 2:* Captain Charles B. Hall is first Tuskegee pilot to shoot down an enemy aircraft

October: 99th Fighter Squadron joins 79th Fighter Group

1948 *July 26:* President Harry Truman announces Executive Order 9981, calling for equal treatment and opportunity in U.S. armed forces, regardless of race

1972 Tuskegee Airmen Incorporated is founded

1998 Benjamin O. Davis Jr. achieves rank of four-star general

INDEX (*Boldface* page numbers indicate illustrations.)

PHOTO CREDITS

Photographs ©: Air Education Training Command/History Office, Randolph Air Force Base: 9; Air Force Historical Research Agency, Maxwell Air Force Base: 1, 10, 14, 15, 24 bottom; AP/Wide World Photos: 12, 30 top (U.S. Army Signal Corps), 7; Corbis-Bettmann: 13, 31 center (United Press Photo), 5, 18, 20 (UPI), 11, 30 bottom; Courtesy of Colonel Roosevelt J. Lewis, U.S.A.F.: 26; Marijon Clark: 2; Medals of America Press: 24 top; National Association of Tuskegee Airmen: 28 bottom; National Defense University Library: 4, 31 top; Osprey Publishing Ltd.: 25; Photri-Microstock: 28 top, 31 bottom (Helen Stikkel), cover, 23; Stock Montage, Inc.: 6; White House Historical Association: 27.

Maps by TJS Design.

PICTURE IDENTIFICATIONS

Cover: The 99th Pursuit Squadron poses in front of a P-40. Most of the Tuskegee Airmen did not like flying the P-40 because it was an out-of-date plane.
Page 1: The first African-American pilots listen to their instructor, Lieutenant R.M. Long (far left). The cadets are, from left to right: George "Spanky" Roberts, Benjamin Davis Jr., Charles DeBow, Mac Ross, and Lemuel Rodney Custis.
Page 2: This statue of a Tuskegee Airman is at the United States Air Force Academy, in Colorado Springs, Colorado.

ABOUT THE AUTHOR

Charles and Linda George are former teachers who have authored more than two dozen nonfiction books for children and young adults. For Children's Press, they have written for several series, including Cornerstones of Freedom, Community Builders, and America the Beautiful, Second Series.